Underground
H A B I T A T S

BY ARNOLD RINGSTAD

Published by The Child's World®
1980 Lookout Drive • Mankato, MN 56003-1705
800-599-READ • www.childsworld.com

Acknowledgments
The Child's World®: Mary Berendes, Publishing Director
Red Line Editorial: Editorial direction
The Design Lab: Design
Amnet: Production

Photographs ©: Marcin Pawinski/Shutterstock Images,
cover, 1; Shutterstock Images, back cover, 10, 13,
21, 23; Eric Isselee/Shutterstock Images, back cover;
Igor Stramyk/Shutterstock Images, 5; Denis and Yulia
Pogostins/Shutterstock Images, 6–7; iStockphoto/
Thinkstock, 8–9; Jason Mintzer/Shutterstock Images,
14–15; Ian Rentoul/Shutterstock Images, 16;
National Park Service, 18–19

ISBN 9781623239923
LCCN 2013947270

Printed in the United States of America
Mankato, MN
December, 2013
PA02192

Table of Contents

Life Under Your Feet

You see animals every day. They walk on the ground. They also fly through the air. But many animals are harder to see. They dig and crawl under the ground. Underground animals enjoy their cool, dark habitats. Underground plants have peaceful places to grow.

Both animals and plants make their homes underground. They live, eat, and grow there. They also help each other survive. Animals bring fresh air to plants by digging through the soil. Plants are eaten as food by other animals.

Underground habitats are in danger. Some human activities harm **prairies** and **wetlands**. This also harms plants and animals. Periods without rainfall can also damage these habitats. It is hard for underground life to survive when the soil is dry.

Although it is hard to see, there are many plants and animals that make their homes underground.

Beneath the Earth

There is a hidden world under our feet. Life exists under the ground all across Earth. These animals and plants live in soil. Soil usually goes from the surface to about 3 feet (1 m) below ground. This small space contains many different kinds of life.

Many plants and animals do not spend their entire life underground. Plants have parts below ground. They also have parts above ground. Some animals only go underground to sleep.

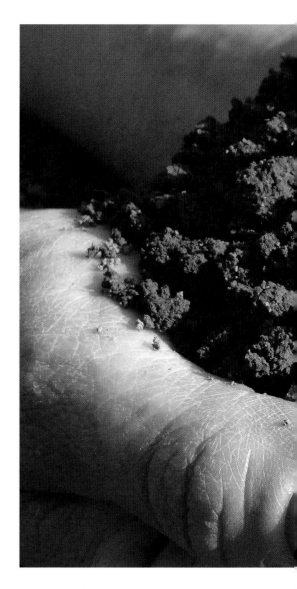

Soil is home for many different forms of life.

Others go to escape danger. Some animals live underground all the time. They hardly peek above ground.

Many animals that live below ground use their sense of touch more than their sense of sight.

In the Dirt

Soil is a home for underground plants and animals. It is a mix of **minerals** and organic matter. Minerals include sand, **silt**, and clay. Organic matter includes dead plants or animals. It provides **nutrients** for plants to grow.

Many things happen to create soil. First, minerals must be in the ground. Then, plants and animals must die to create organic matter. Weather can also affect the creation of soil. Rainfall and wind wear away soil. They also carry minerals to new places. Weather has big effects on the earth over time.

Big pieces of minerals are called rocks. Most rocks are made from **magma**. Magma is melted rock that flows from beneath the earth's surface. Other rocks are made from layers of minerals. These minerals join together

Some rocks are made from minerals. These minerals create layers in the rock.

over time. Large rocks above ground can become shelters for animals. Animals can hide beneath the rocks for protection from wind and rain.

How's the Weather Down There?

The sun's rays do not reach underground. Rain, snow, and wind do not reach there either. This means temperatures a few feet below the ground do not change much. Underground temperatures around the world are not the same. But in each area, the underground temperature is about the same all year.

Animals escape many kinds of weather underground. It helps that the temperature is the same. Desert animals can dig to keep cool. Arctic animals can dig to keep warm. Other animals can dig to escape winds and storms.

The temperature also makes it easy to live underground. Plants and animals do not get too hot or cold. Both plants and animals need one thing to live, however. They need water. The soil they live in needs to have moisture in it.

Some desert animals dig holes below ground to escape the hot sun.

11

Underground Plants and Mushrooms

Many amazing plants and **mushrooms** grow underground. Some stay below ground. Other plants grow some parts below ground and some above ground. Underground plants and mushrooms help other plants grow. When they die, their organic matter becomes food for new plants.

Most truffle mushrooms are found in Europe and Asia.

One kind of mushroom lives entirely underground. It is called a truffle. Many people love the taste of truffles. Chefs use them as part of fancy dishes. Truffles can be hard to find underground. Farmers use pigs to help. The pigs sniff out and dig up this uncommon mushroom.

Turnips are plants that live partly underground. The bulb-shaped root is below ground. The green, leafy part of a turnip grows above ground. The root is the part people eat. People have been picking and eating turnips for 15,000 years!

Farmers must dig below ground to find truffle mushrooms.

Crawling through the Earth

Animals use their underground habitats in different ways. Some go underground to escape the weather. Some dig to escape **predators**. And others dig to find food.

Garter snakes go underground to escape cold weather. They like warm temperatures. Garter snakes **hibernate**. They dig underground pits. Many garter snakes go into one pit. They stay close together to keep warm.

Earthworms live in the dirt. They live in North America, Europe, and Asia. Earthworms eat nutrients from the dirt as they crawl through it. Earthworms are an important food for many animals. Birds, toads, and rats eat them. People also use earthworms as bait for fishing.

Gartner snakes move below ground when temperatures become colder.

Termites are small bugs that look like ants. Some termites live underground. They are found in every U.S. state except Alaska. It is too cold there for them to live. These bugs build huge underground colonies. Termites eat wood. They turn it into soil called **humus**. Humus holds more nutrients than regular soil. This soil is good for plants living near a termite colony.

Underground Homes

Some mammals also build their homes underground. They dig tunnels. Here they can rest or keep their babies safe. They can also eat. Hidden homes keep them away from predators.

The average groundhog weighs 13 pounds (6 kg).

Groundhogs live in the northeastern United States and Canada. They look like large squirrels. Groundhogs dig huge dens. They have many different entrances. These tunnels keep predators from finding the groundhogs.

Voles also dig dens. These small animals look like mice. They live in North America, Europe, and Asia. Voles also build many entrances to hide from predators. They often build their tunnels beneath plants. When they are in the tunnels they eat the plants' roots.

Voles check the entrance of their tunnels for predators before coming up from underground.

The Star-Nosed Mole

The star-nosed mole is a special animal. It has learned to live in its underground habitat. Moles like to live in wet soil. Moles are the size of a hamster. They dig through the soil to find food. They are also good at swimming. Some moles dig tunnels that open into lakes and streams.

The star-nosed mole has feelers around its nose. This is where it got its name. These touchy feelers have many uses. They keep dirt from going in a mole's nose. The feelers also find food. All 22 feelers search around the mole. When one touches something, the mole can quickly figure out what it is. The mole eats the object if it is food.

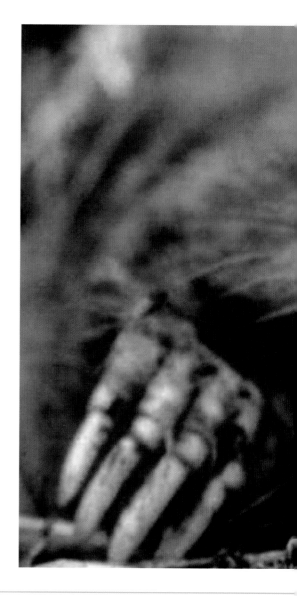

Star-nosed moles live in the eastern United States and Canada.

Star-nosed moles also help farmers and plants. They eat bugs that eat farmers' crops. Digging tunnels is also good for the soil. It brings fresh air to plants' roots. Fresh air helps plants grow.

Threats to Underground Habitats

Underground habitats are found across the world. Some underground habitats are in danger. These dangers can harm plants and animals that live there.

Star-nosed moles live in and underneath wetlands. Builders are clearing many wetlands. This makes space for homes or other buildings. When wetlands disappear, moles have no place to live.

Voles dig their tunnels under prairies. But many prairie areas are in danger. Farmers use prairies to plant their crops. They also let their animals eat the prairie grasses. Too much of this can kill prairie plants. This includes the plants that voles eat. When their food and land disappears, the voles will not survive.

Animals are not the only things in danger in underground habitats. Plants and mushrooms are also in trouble. Truffles need wet soil to survive. But **droughts** can dry out the soil. The truffles cannot grow when this happens.

Humans must take care of underground habitats. Even though they are hard to see, the plants and animals living there need safe homes.

A drought can be harmful to plants and animals that live underground.

GLOSSARY

droughts (DROUTS) Droughts are long periods of time without rain. Droughts dry out the ground.

hibernate (HYE-bur-nate) To hibernate is to sleep for several months through the winter. Garter snakes hibernate.

humus (HYOO-muhss) Humus is soil that is good at holding nutrients. Termites turn soil into humus.

magma (MAG-muh) Hot, melted rocks inside Earth are called magma. Most rocks are made from magma.

minerals (MIN-ur-uhls) Minerals are natural substances found in the ground. Soil has minerals in it.

mushrooms (MUHSH-rooms) Mushrooms are fungi that grow above and below ground. A truffle is a special mushroom.

nutrients (noo-tree-uhnts) Nutrients are matter that living things need to grow. Earthworms eat nutrients from the soil.

prairies (PRAIR-ees) Prairies are flat or rolling land with grass. Voles live under prairies.

predators (PRE-duh-turz) Predators are animals that hunt and eat other animals. Bears are predators.

silt (SILT) Silt is very small particles left from water. Silt is a mineral.

wetlands (WET-landz) Wetlands are areas soaked with water. Star-nosed moles live near wetlands.

TO LEARN MORE

BOOKS

George, Lynn. *Termites: Mound Builders (Animal Architects)*. New York: PowerKids Press, 2010.

Kalman, Bobbie. *Underground Habitats (Introducing Habitats)*. New York: Crabtree, 2007.

Sebastian, Emily. *Moles (Animals Underground)*. New York: PowerKids Press, 2011.

WEB SITES

Visit our Web site for links about underground habitats:
childsworld.com/links

Note to Parents, Teachers, and Librarians: We routinely verify our Web links to make sure they are safe and active sites. So encourage your readers to check them out!

INDEX

ABOUT THE AUTHOR

Arnold Ringstad lives in Minnesota. He likes to visit the local zoo so he can see animals from all kinds of habitats.